DOT TO [DOT]
FOR KIDS

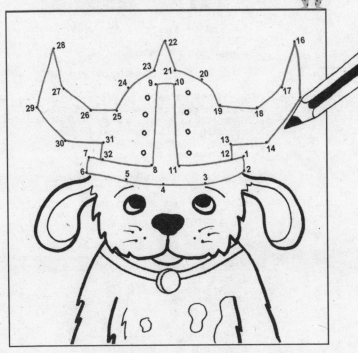

Puzzles by
Emily Golden Twomey

Buster Books

First published in Great Britain in 2021
by Buster Books, an imprint of Michael O'Mara Books Limited,
9 Lion Yard, Tremadoc Road, London SW4 7NQ

The material in this book was previously published in *Buster's Brilliant Dot to Dot*,
The Kids' Book of Dot to Dot and *The Kids' Book of Dot to Dot 1*

 www.mombooks.com/buster Buster Books @BusterBooks 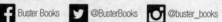 @buster_books

Copyright © Buster Books 2013, 2015, 2017, 2021

Puzzles by Emily Golden Twomey

Illustrations by John Bigwood

A CIP catalogue record for this book is available from the British Library.

ISBN: 978-1-78055-835-6

1 3 5 7 9 10 8 6 4 2

Papers used by Buster Books are natural, recyclable products made of wood from
well-managed, FSC®-certified forests and other controlled sources. The manufacturing
processes conform to the environmental regulations of the country of origin.

Printed and bound in November 2021 by CPI Group (UK) Ltd,
108 Beddington Lane, Croydon CR0 4YY, United Kingdom

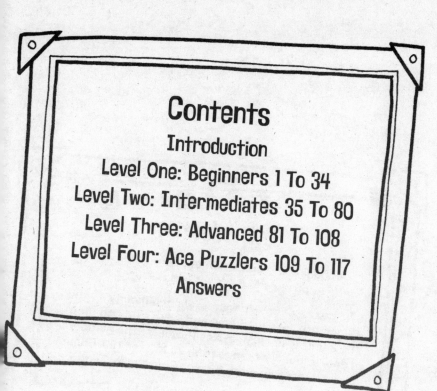

Contents

Introduction

Answers

Introduction

A challenging collection of connect-the-dot puzzles to discover and colour.

The puzzles come in four levels of difficulty – with Beginners, Intermediates and Advanced and then the ultimate challenge, Ace Puzzlers. The number of dots to connect range from 20 to over 100. Some pictures contain more than one puzzle challenge.

The answers are at the back if you get lost and need to take a sneak peak to get back on track.

Level One:

Beginners

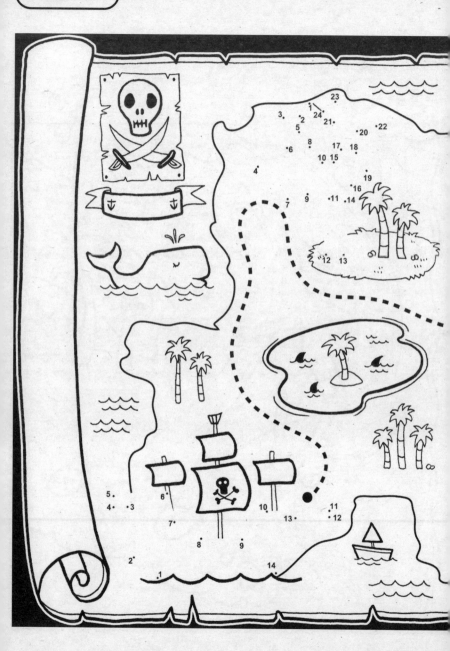

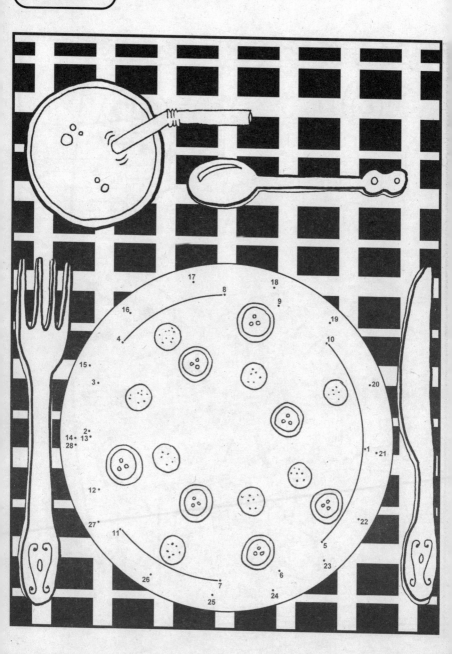

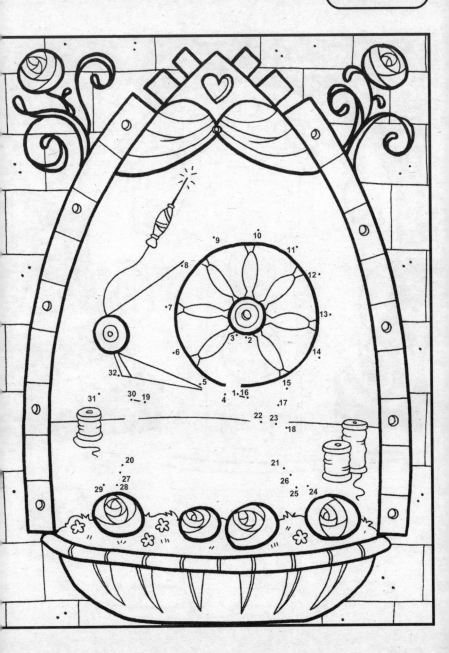

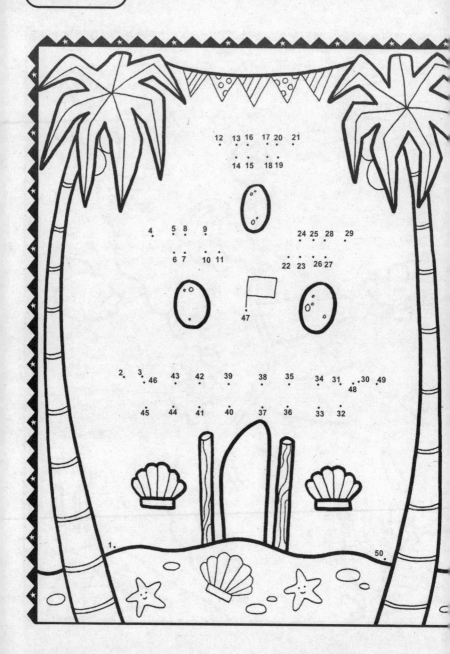

Puzzle 27

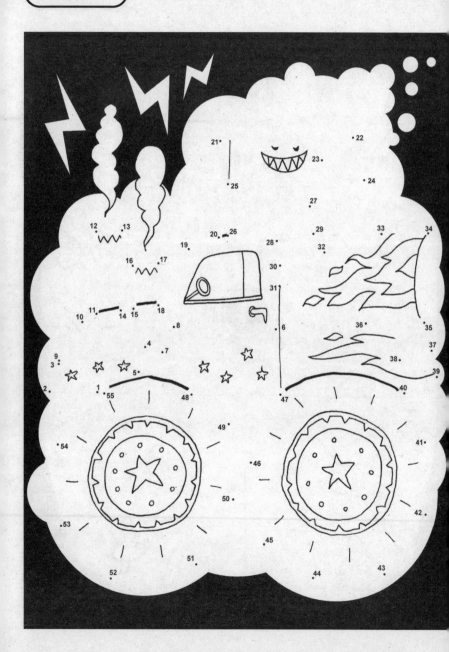

Level Two:

Intermediates

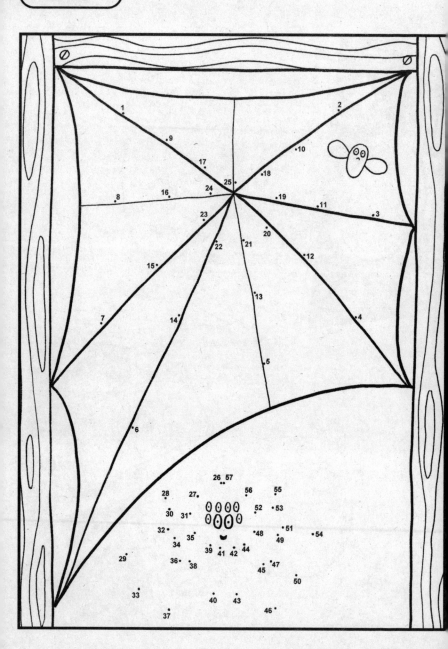

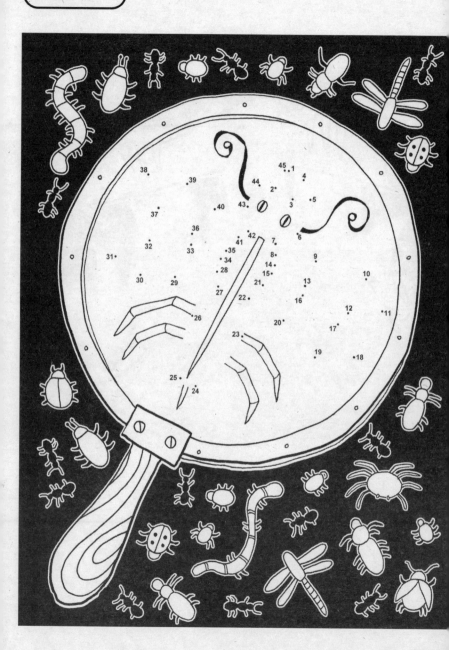

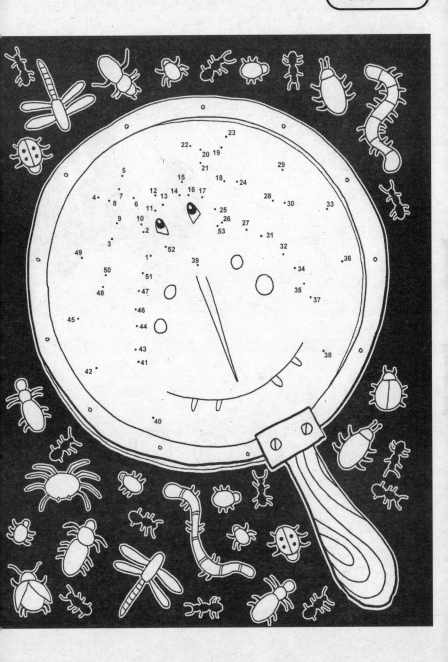

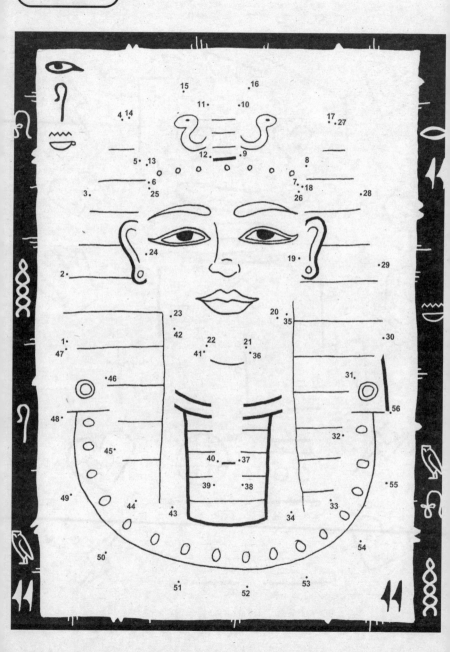

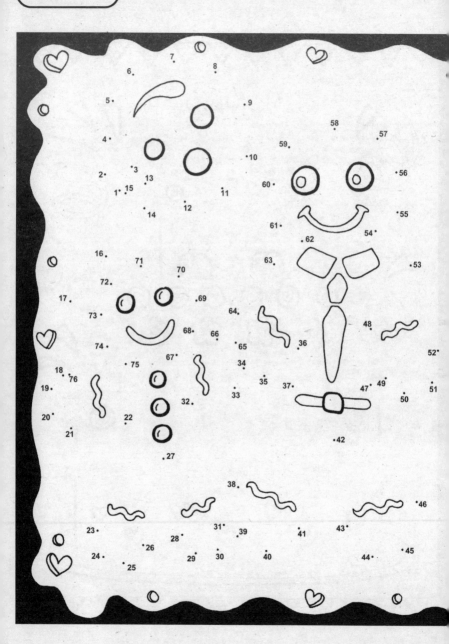

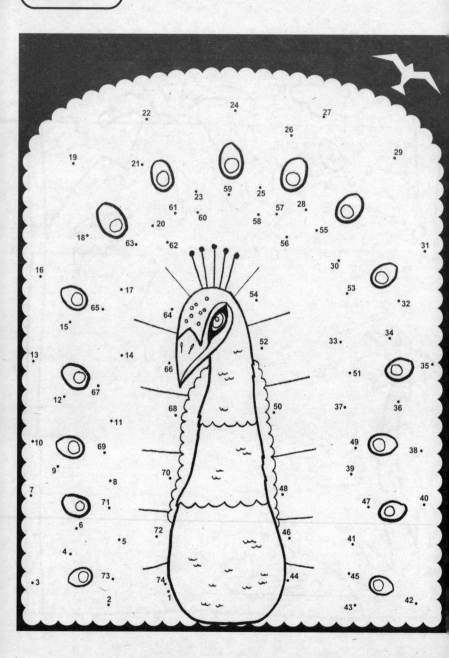

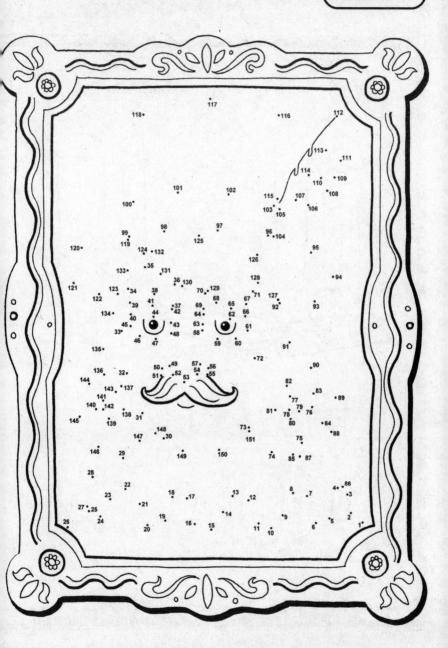

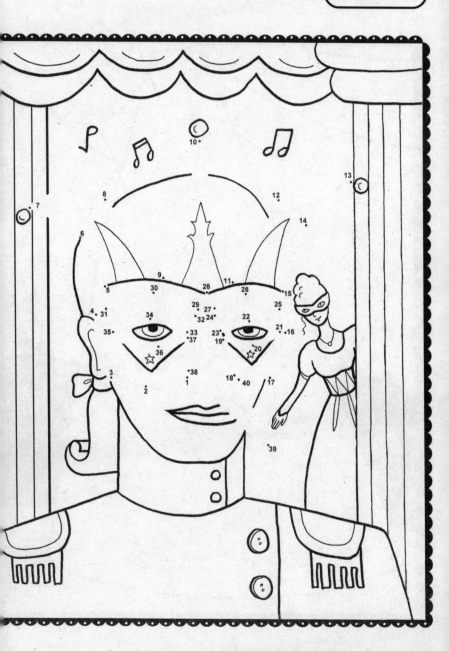

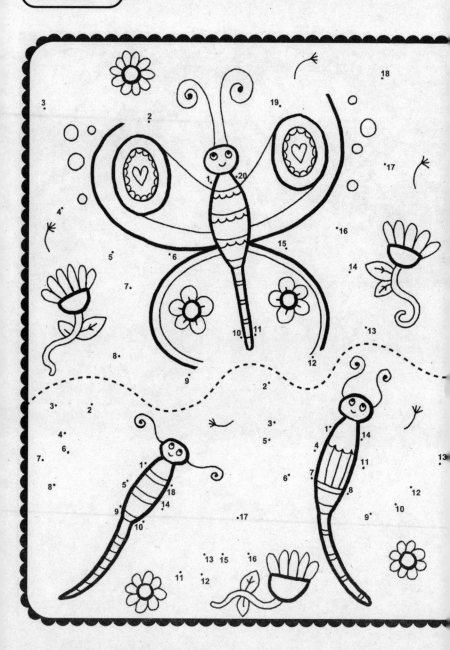

Level Three:
Advanced

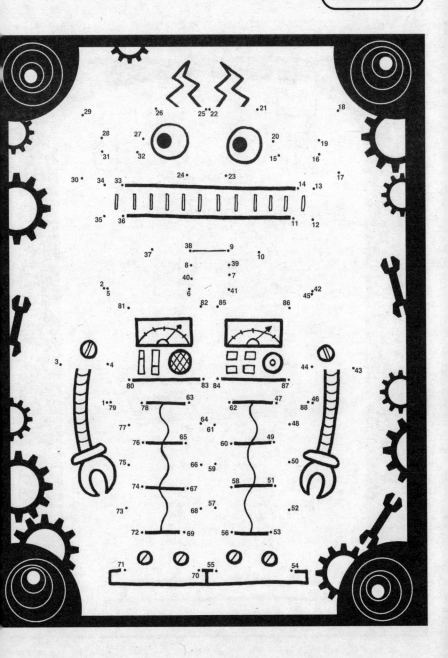

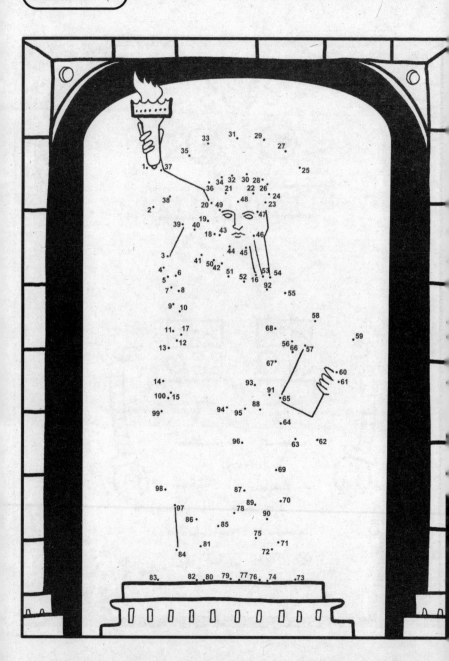

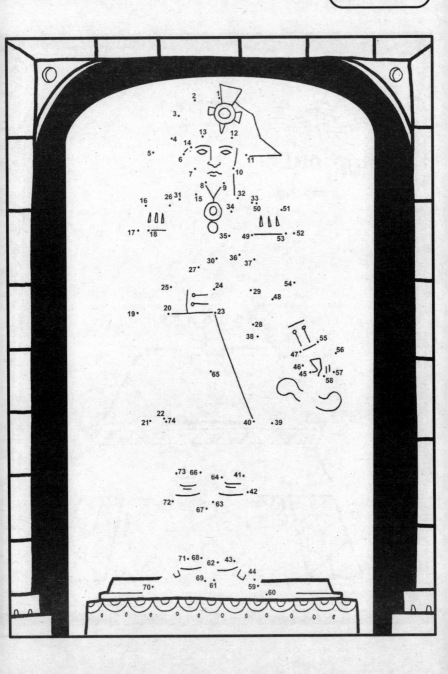

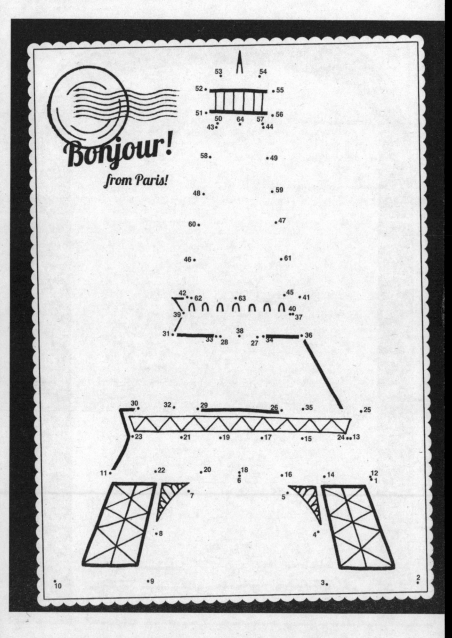

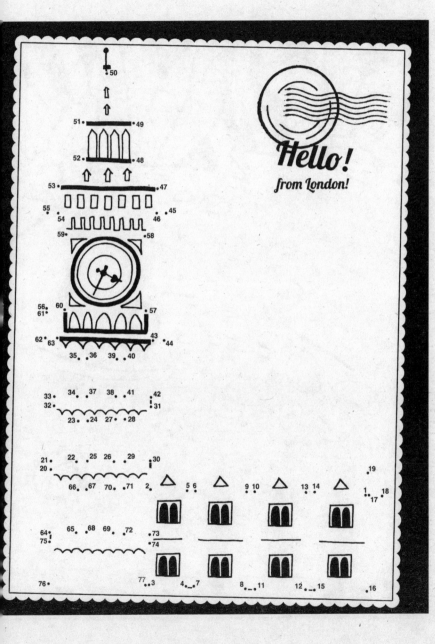

Hello!
from London!

Puzzle 93

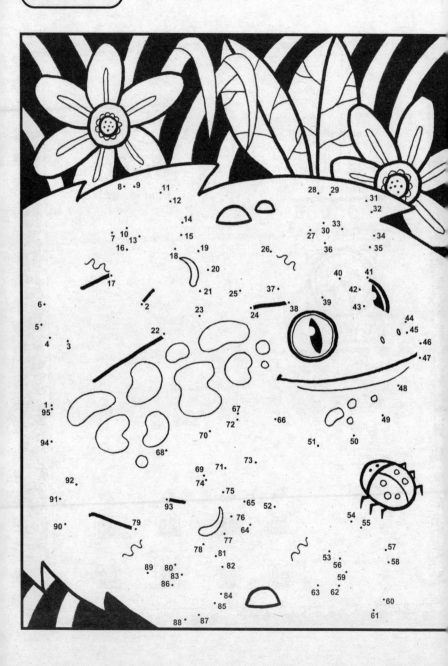

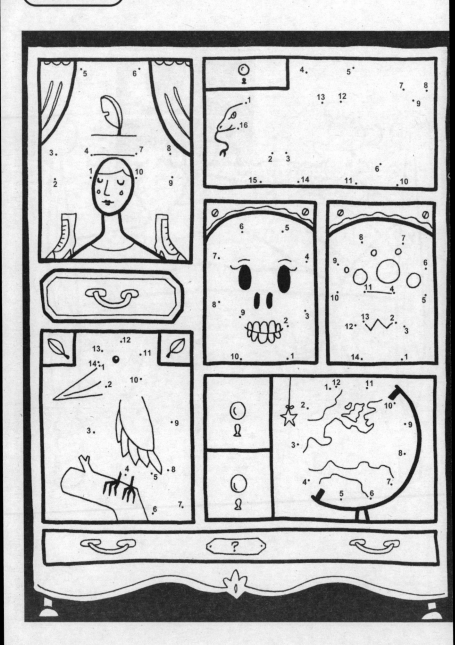

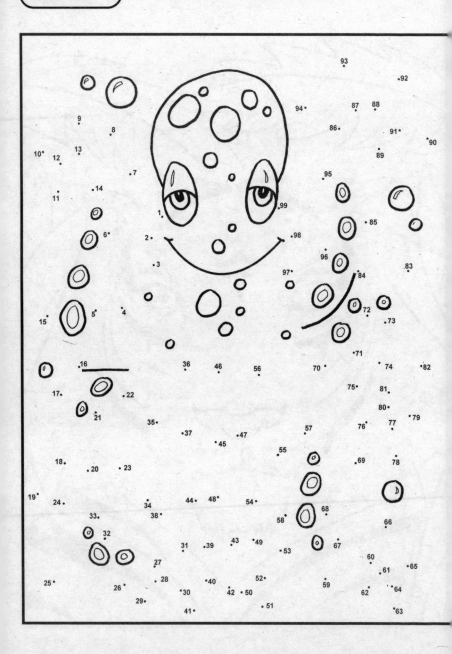

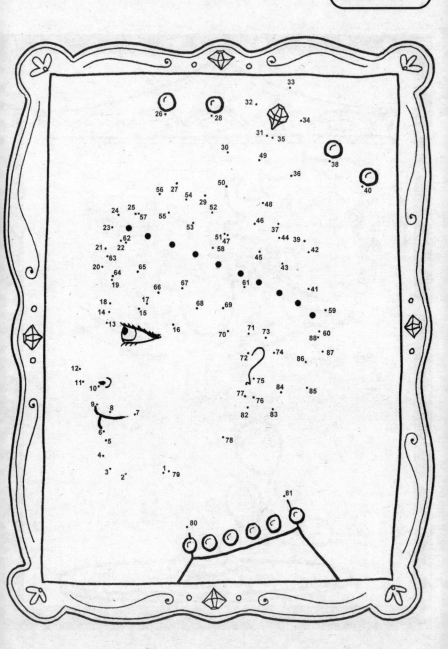

Level Four:
Ace Puzzlers

Puzzle 109

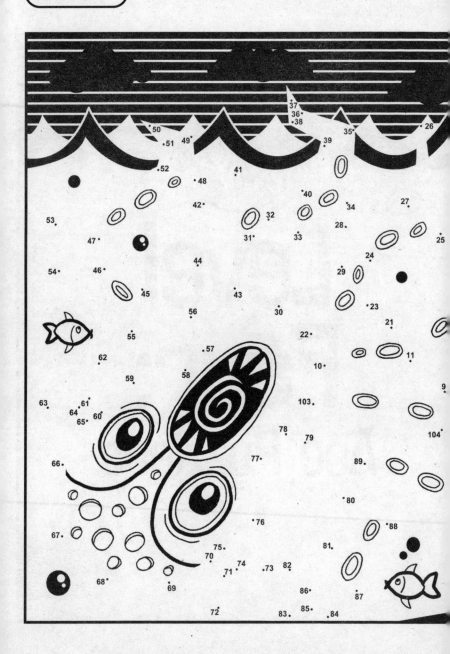

Puzzle 114

Answers

Beginners

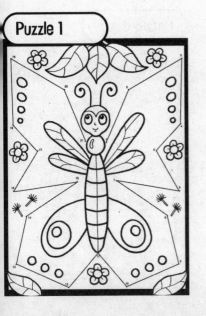

Puzzle 3

Puzzle 4

Puzzle 5

Puzzle 6

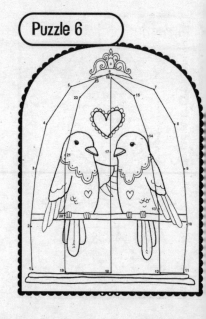

Puzzle 7

Puzzle 8

Puzzle 9

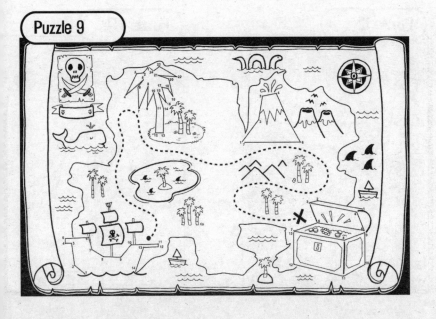

Puzzle 10

Puzzle 11

Puzzle 12

Puzzle 13

Puzzle 14

Puzzle 15

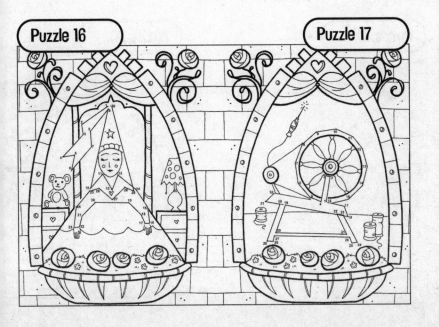

Puzzle 16

Puzzle 17

Puzzle 18

Puzzle 19

Puzzle 20

Puzzle 21

Puzzle 22

Puzzle 23

Puzzle 24

Puzzle 25

Puzzle 26

Puzzle 27

Puzzle 28

Puzzle 29

Puzzle 30

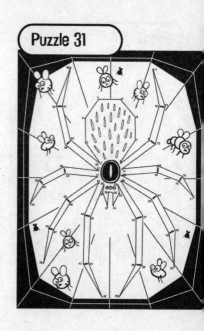

Puzzle 31

Puzzle 32

Puzzle 33

Puzzle 34

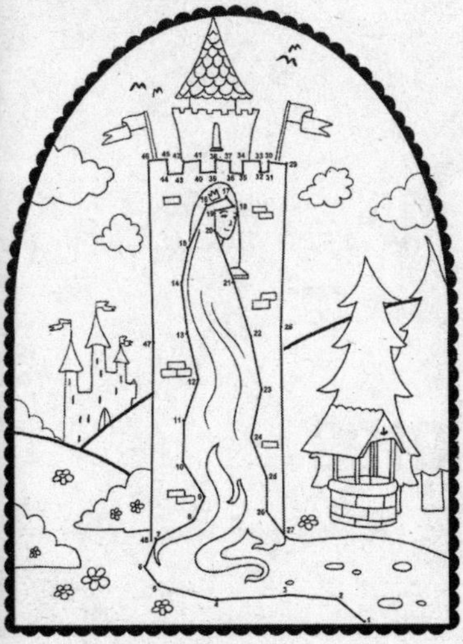

Intermediates

Puzzle 36

Puzzle 37

Puzzle 38

Puzzle 39

Puzzle 40

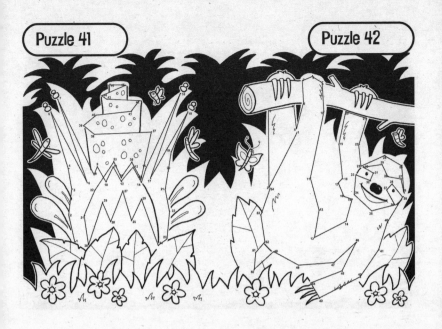

Puzzle 41   Puzzle 42

Puzzle 43   Puzzle 44

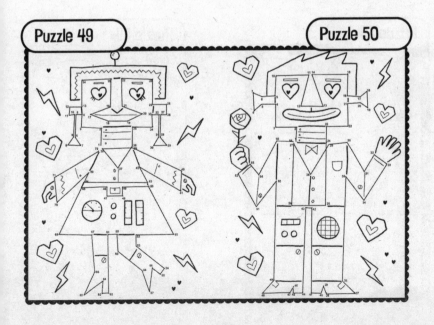

Puzzle 51

Puzzle 52

Puzzle 53

Puzzle 54

Puzzle 55

Puzzle 56

Puzzle 57

Puzzle 58

Puzzle 59

Puzzle 60

Puzzle 61

Puzzle 62

Puzzle 63

Puzzle 64

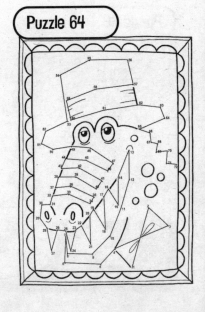

Puzzle 65

Puzzle 66

Puzzle 67

Puzzle 68

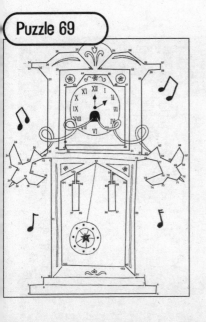

Puzzle 69

Puzzle 70

Puzzle 71

Puzzle 72

Puzzle 73

Puzzle 74

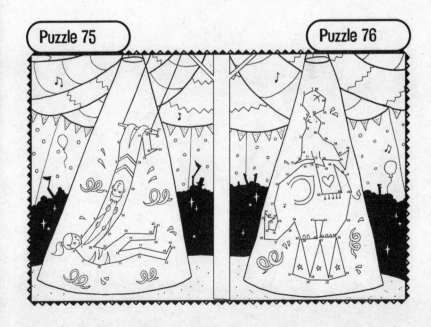

Puzzle 75

Puzzle 76

Puzzle 77

Puzzle 78

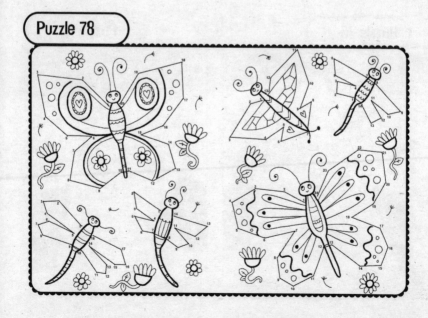

Puzzle 79

Puzzle 80

Advanced

Puzzle 82

Puzzle 83

Puzzle 84

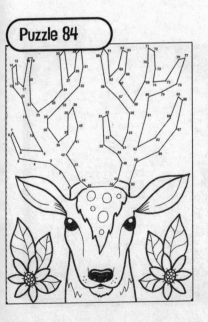

Puzzle 85

Puzzle 86

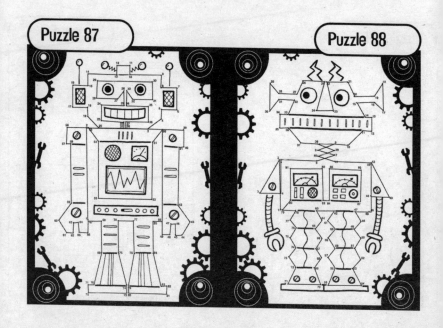

Puzzle 87

Puzzle 88

Puzzle 89

Puzzle 90

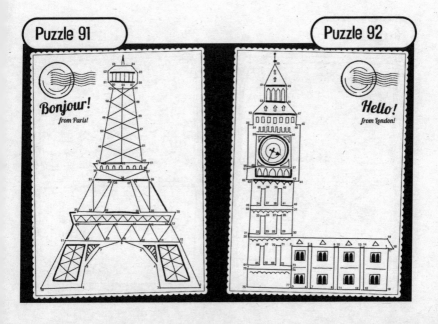

Puzzle 91

Bonjour!
from Paris!

Puzzle 92

Hello!
from London!

Puzzle 93

Puzzle 94

Puzzle 95

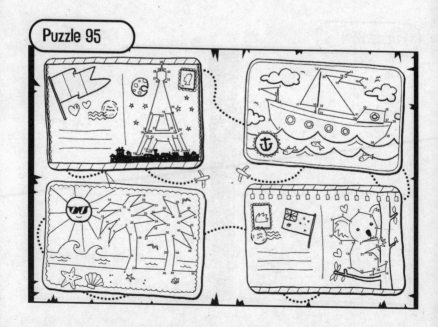

Puzzle 96

Puzzle 97

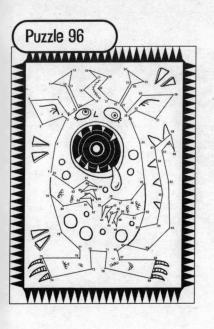

Puzzle 98

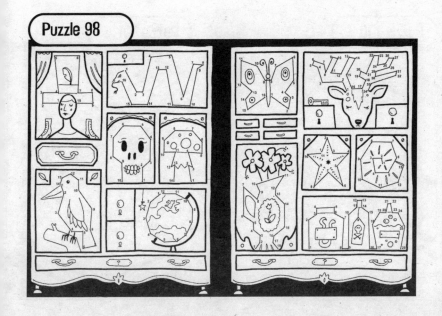

Puzzle 99

Puzzle 100

Puzzle 101

Puzzle 102

Puzzle 103

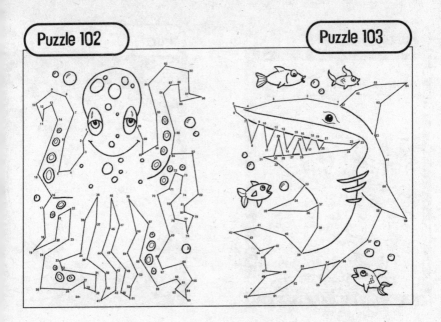

Puzzle 104

Puzzle 105

Puzzle 106

Puzzle 107

Puzzle 108

Ace Puzzlers

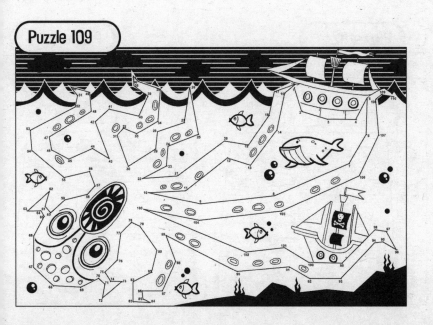

Puzzle 110

Puzzle 111

Puzzle 112

Puzzle 113

Puzzle 114

Puzzle 115

Puzzle 116

Puzzle 117